SHAKESPEARE'S BONES

THE PROPOSAL TO DISINTER THEM,
CONSIDERED IN RELATION TO THEIR POSSIBLE
BEARING ON HIS PORTRAITURE:
ILLUSTRATED BY INSTANCES OF VISITS OF THE
LIVING TO THE DEAD.

C. M. Ingleby, LL.D., V.P.R.S.L.,

Honorary Member of the German Shakespeare Society, and a
Life-Trustee of Shakespeare's Birthplace, Museum, and New
Place, at Stratford-upon-Avon.

1st WORLD
LIBRARY
Literary Society

Shakespeare's Bones

C. M. Ingleby

© 1st World Library – Literary Society, 2004
PO Box 2211
Fairfield, IA 52556
www.1stworldlibrary.org
First Edition

LCCN: 2004091167

Softcover ISBN: 1-59540-613-1
eBook ISBN: 1-59540-713-8

Purchase *"Shakespeare's Bones"*
as a traditional bound book at:
www.1stWorldLibrary.org/purchase.asp?ISBN=1-59540-613-1

"Let's talk of graves, of worms, and epitaphs."
Richard II, a. iii, s. 2.

This Essay is respectfully inscribed to The Major and Corporation of Stratford-upon-Avon, and the Vicar of the Church of the Holy Trinity there, by their friend and colleague,

THE AUTHOR.

SHAKESPEARE'S BONES.

The sentiment which affects survivors in the disposition of their dead, and which is, in one regard, a superstition, is, in another, a creditable outcome of our common humanity: namely, the desire to honour the memory of departed worth, and to guard the "hallowed reliques" by the erection of a shrine, both as a visible mark of respect for the dead, and as a place of resort for those pilgrims who may come to pay him tribute. It is this sentiment which dots our graveyards with memorial tablets and more ambitious sculptures, and which still preserves so many of our closed churchyards from desecration, and our {1a} ancient tombs from the molestation of careless, curious, or mercenary persons.

But there is another sentiment, not inconsistent with this, which prompts us, on suitable occasions, to disinter the remains of great men, and remove them to a more fitting and more honourable resting-place. The Hotel des Invalides at Paris, and the Basilica of San Lorenzo Fuori le Mura at Rome, {1b} are indebted to this sentiment for the possession of relics which make those edifices the natural resort of pilgrims as of sight-seers. It were a work of superfluity to adduce further illustration of the position that the mere exhumation and reinterment of a great man's remains, is commonly held to be, in special cases, a justifiable proceeding, not a violation of that honourable sentiment of humanity, which protects and consecrates the depositaries of the dead. On a late occasion it was not the belief that such a proceeding is a violation of our more sacred instincts which hindered the removal to Pennsylvania of the remains of William Penn; but simply the belief that they had already a more suitable resting-place in his native land. {2}

There is still another sentiment, honourable in itself and not inconsistent with those which I have specified, though still more conditional upon the sufficiency of the reasons conducing to the act: namely, the desire, by exhumation, to set at rest a reasonable or important issue respecting the person of the deceased while he was yet a living man. Accordingly it is held justifiable to exhume a body recently buried, in order to discover the cause of death, or to settle a question of disputed identity: nor is it usually held unjustifiable to exhume a body long since deceased, in order to find such evidences as time may not have wholly destroyed, of his personal appearance, including the size and shape of his head, and the special characteristics of his living face.

It is too late for the most reverential and scrupulous to object to this as an invasion of the sanctity of the grave, or a violation of the rights of the dead or of the feelings of his family. When a man has been long in the grave, there are probably no family feelings to be wounded by such an act: and, as for his rights, if he can be said to have any, we may surely reckon among them the right of not being supposed to possess such objectionable personal defects as may have been imputed to him by the malice of critics or by the incapacity of sculptor or painter, and which his remains may be sufficiently unchanged to rebut: in a word we owe him something more than refraining from disturbing his remains until they are undistinguishable from the earth in which they lie, a debt which no supposed inviolable sanctity of the grave ought to prevent us from paying.

It is, I say, too late to raise such an objection, because exhumation has been performed many times with a perfectly legitimate object, even in the case of our most illustrious dead, without protest or objection from the most sensitive person. As the examples, more or less analogous to that of Shakespeare, which I am about to adduce, concern great men who were born and were buried within the limits of our island, I will preface them by giving the very extraordinary cases of Schiller and Raphael, which illustrate both classes: those in which the object of the exhumation was to give the remains a more honourable sepulture, and those in which it was purely to resolve certain questions affecting the skull of the deceased. The following is abridged from Mr. Andrew Hamilton's narrative, entitled "The Story of Schiller's Life," published in Macmillan's Magazine for May, 1863.

"At the time of his death Schiller left his widow and children almost penniless, and almost friendless too. The duke and duchess were absent; Goethe lay ill; even Schiller's brother-in-law Wolzogen was away from home. Frau von Wolzogen was with her sister, but seems to have been equally ill-fitted to bear her share of the load that had fallen so heavily upon them. Heinrich Voss was the only friend admitted to the sickroom; and when all was over it was he who went to the joiner's, and, knowing the need of economy, ordered 'a plain deal coffin.' It cost ten shillings of our money.

"In the early part of 1805, one Carl Leberecht Schwabe, an enthusiastic admirer of Schiller, left Weimar on business. Returning on Saturday the 11th of May, between three and four in the afternoon, his first errand was to visit his betrothed, who lived in the house adjoining that of the Schillers. She met him in the passage, and told him, Schiller was two days dead, and that night he was to be buried. On putting further questions, Schwabe stood aghast at what he learned. The funeral was to be private and to take place immediately after midnight, without any religious rite. Bearers had been hired to carry the remains to the churchyard, and no one else was to attend.

"Schwabe felt that all this could not go on; but to prevent it was difficult. There were but eight hours left; and the arrangements, such as they were, had already been made. However, he went straight to the house of death, and requested an interview with Frau von Schiller. She replied, through the servant, 'that she was too greatly overwhelmed by her loss to be able to see or speak to any one; as for the funeral of her blessed husband, Mr. Schwabe must apply to the Reverend Oberconsistorialrath Gunther, who had kindly undertaken to see done what was necessary; whatever he might direct, she would approve of.' With this message Schwabe hastened to Gunther, and told him, his blood boiled at the thought that Schiller should be borne to the grave by hirelings. At first Gunther shook his head and said, 'It was too late; everything was arranged; the bearers were already ordered.' Schwabe offered to become responsible for the payment of the bearers, if they were dismissed. At length the Oberconsistorialrath inquired who the gentlemen were who had agreed to bear the coffin. Schwabe was obliged to acknowledge that he could not

C. M. Ingleby

at that moment mention a single name; but he was ready to guarantee his Hochwurde that in an hour or two he would bring him the list. On this his Hochwurde consented to countermand the bearers.

"Schwabe now rushed from house to house, obtaining a ready assent from all whom he found at home. But as some were out, he sent round a circular, begging those who would come to place a mark against their names. He requested them to meet at his lodgings 'at half-past twelve o'clock that night; a light would be placed in the window to guide those who were not acquainted with the house; they would be kind enough to be dressed in black; but mourning-hats, crapes and mantles he had already provided.' Late in the evening he placed the list in Gunther's hands. Several appeared to whom he had not applied; in all about twenty.

"Between midnight and one in the morning the little band proceeded to Schiller's house. The coffin was carried down stairs and placed on the shoulders of the friends in waiting. No one else was to be seen before the house or in the streets. It was a moonlight night in May, but clouds were up. The procession moved through the sleeping city to the churchyard of St. James. Having arrived there they placed their burden on the ground at the door of the so-called Kassengewolbe, where the gravedigger and his assistants took it up. In this vault, which belonged to the province of Weimar, it was usual to inter persons of the higher classes, who possessed no burying-ground of their own, upon payment of a louis d'or. As Schiller had died without securing a resting-place for himself and his family, there could have been no more natural arrangement than to carry his remains to this vault. It was a grim old building, standing against the wall of the churchyard, with a steep narrow roof, and no opening of any kind but the doorway which was filled up with a grating. The interior was a gloomy space of about fourteen feet either way. In the centre was a trap-door which gave access to a hollow space beneath.

"As the gravediggers raised the coffin, the clouds suddenly parted, and the moon shed her light on all that was earthly of Schiller. They carried him in: they opened the trap-door: and let him down by ropes into the darkness. Then they closed the vault. Nothing was spoken or sung. The mourners were dispersing, when their attention was attracted by a tall figure in a mantle, at some distance in the graveyard, sobbing loudly. No one knew who it was; and for many years the occurrence remained wrapped in mystery, giving rise to strange conjectures. But eventually it turned out to have been Schiller's brother-in-law Wolzogen, who, having hurried home on hearing of the death, had arrived after the procession was already on its way to the churchyard.

"In the year 1826, Schwabe was Burgermeister of Weimar. Now it was the custom of the Landschafts-collegium, or provincial board under whose jurisdiction this institution was placed, to CLEAR OUT the Kassengewolbe from time to time - whenever it was found to be inconveniently crowded - and by this means to make way for other deceased persons and more louis d'or. On such occasions - when the Landschaftscollegium gave the order 'aufzuraumen,' it was the usage to dig a hole in a corner of the churchyard - then to bring up en masse the contents of the Kassengewolbe - coffins, whether entire or in fragments, bones, skulls, and tattered graveclothes -

and finally to shovel the whole heap into the aforesaid pit. In the month of March Schwabe was dismayed at hearing that the Landschaftscollegium had decreed a speedy 'clearing out' of the Gewolbe. His old prompt way of acting had not left him; he went at once to his friend Weyland, the president of the Collegium. 'Friend Weyland,' he said, 'let not the dust of Schiller be tossed up in the face of heaven and flung into that hideous hole! Let me at least have a permit to search the vault; if we find Schiller's coffin, it shall be reinterred in a fitting manner in the New Cemetery.' The president made no difficulty.

"Schwabe invited several persons who had known the poet, and amongst others one Rudolph, who had been Schiller's servant at the time of his death. On March 13th, at four o'clock in the afternoon, the party met in the churchyard, the sexton and his assistants having received orders to be present with keys, ladders, &c. The vault was opened; but, before any one entered it, Rudolph and another stated that the coffin of the deceased Hofrath von Schiller must be one of the longest in the place. After this the secretary of the Landschaftscollegium was requested to read aloud from the records of the said board the names of such persons as had been interred shortly before and after the year 1805. This being done, the gravedigger Bielke remarked that the coffins no longer lay in the order in which they had originally been placed, but had been displaced at recent burials. The ladder was then adjusted, and Schwabe, Coudray the architect, and the gravedigger, were the first to descend. Some others were asked to draw near, that they might assist in recognising the coffin. The first glance brought their hopes very low. The tenants of the vault were found 'over, under and alongside of each other.' One coffin of unusual length having been descried underneath the rest, an attempt was made to reach it by lifting out of the way those that were above it; but the processes of the tomb were found to have made greater advances than met the eye. Hardly anything would bear removal, but fell to pieces at the first touch. Search was made for plates with inscriptions, but even the metal plates crumbled away on being fingered, and their inscriptions were utterly effaced. Two plates only were found with legible characters, and these were foreign to the purpose. Probably every one but the Burgermeister looked on the matter as hopeless. They reascended the ladder and closed the vault.

"Meanwhile these strange proceedings in the Kassengewolbe began to be noised abroad. The churchyard was a thoroughfare, and many passengers had observed that something unusual was going on. There were persons living in Weimar whose near relatives lay in the Gewolbe; and, though neither they nor the public at large had any objection to offer to the general 'clearing out,' they did raise very strong objections to this mode of anticipating it. So many pungent things began to be said about violating the tomb, disturbing the repose of the departed, &c., that the Burgermeister perceived the necessity of going more warily to work in future. He resolved to time his next visit at an hour when few persons would be likely to cross the churchyard at that season. Accordingly, two days later he returned to the Kassengewolbe at seven in the morning, accompanied only by Coudray and the churchyard officials.

"Their first task was to raise out of the vault altogether six coffins, which it was found would bear removal. By various tokens it was proved that none of these could be that of which they were in search. There were several others which could not be removed, but which held together so long as they were left where they lay. All the rest were in the direst confusion. Two hours and a half were spent in subjecting the ghastly heap to a thorough but fruitless search: not a trace of any kind rewarded their trouble. Only one conclusion stared Schwabe and Coudray in the face - their quest was in vain: the remains of Schiller must be left to oblivion. Again the Gewolbe was closed, and those who had disturbed its quiet returned disappointed to their homes. Yet, that very afternoon, Schwabe went back once more in company with the joiner who twenty years before had made the coffin: there was a chance that he might recognise one of those which they had not ventured to raise. But this glimmer of hope faded like all the rest. The man remembered very well what sort of coffin he had made for the Hofrath von Schiller, and he certainly saw nothing like it here. It had been of the plainest sort, he believed without even a plate; and in such damp as this it could have lasted but a few years.

"The fame of this second expedition got abroad like that of the first, and the comments of the public were louder than before. Invectives of no measured sort fell on the mayor in torrents. Not only did society in general take offence, but a variety of persons in authority, particularly ecclesiastical dignitaries, began to talk of interfering. Schwabe was haunted by the idea of the 'clearing out,' which was now close at hand. That dismal hole in the corner of the churchyard once closed and the turf laid down, the dust of Schiller would be lost for ever. He determined to proceed. His position of Burgermeister put the means in his power, and this time he was resolved to keep his secret. To find the skull was now his utmost hope, but for that he would make a final struggle. The keys were still in the hands of Bielke the sexton, who, of course, was under his control. He sent for him, bound him over to silence, and ordered him to be at the churchyard at midnight on the 19th of March. In like manner, he summoned three day-labourers whom he pledged to secrecy, and engaged to meet him at the same place and at the same hour, but singly and without lanterns. Attention should not be attracted if he could help it.

"When the night came, he himself, with a trusty servant, proceeded to the entrance of the Kassenge-wolbe. The four men were already there. In darkness they all entered, raised the trap-door, adjusted the ladder, and descended to the abode of the dead. Not till then were lanterns lighted; it was just possible that some late wanderer might, even at that hour, cross the churchyard. Schwabe seated himself on a step of the ladder and directed the workmen. Fragments of broken coffins they piled up in one corner, and bones in another. Skulls as they were found were placed in a heap by themselves. The work went on from twelve o'clock till about three, for three successive nights, at the end of which time twenty-three skulls had been found. These the Burgermeister caused to be put into a sack and carried to his house, where he himself took them out and placed them in rows on a table.

"It was hardly done ere he exclaimed, 'THAT must be Schiller's!' There was one skull that differed enormously from all the rest, both in size and in shape. It was remarkable, too, in another way: alone of all those on the table it retained an entire set of the finest teeth, and Schiller's teeth had been noted for their beauty. But there were other means of identification at

C. M. Ingleby

hand. Schwabe possessed the cast of Schiller's head, taken after death by Klauer, and with this he undertook to make a careful comparison and measurement. The two seemed to him to correspond, and, of the twenty-two others, not one would bear juxtaposition with the cast. Unfortunately the lower jaw was wanting, to obtain which a fourth nocturnal expedition had to be undertaken. The skull was carried back to the Gewolbe, and many jaws were tried ere one was found which fitted, and for beauty of teeth corresponded with, the upper jaw. When brought home, on the other hand, it refused to fit any other cranium. One tooth alone was wanting, and this was said by an old servant of Schiller's had been extracted at Jena in his presence.

"Having got thus far, Schwabe invited three of the chief medical authorities to inspect his discovery. After careful measurements, they declared that among the twenty-three skulls there was but one from which the cast could have been taken. He then invited every person in Weimar and its neighbourhood, who had been on terms of intimacy with Schiller, and admitted them to the room one by one. The result was surprising. Without an exception they pointed to the same skull as that which must have been the poet's. The only remaining chance of mistake seemed to be the possibility of other skulls having eluded the search, and being yet in the vault. To put this to rest, Schwabe applied to the Landschaftscollegium, in whose records was kept a list of all persons buried in the Kassenge-wolbe. It was ascertained that since the last 'clearing out' there had been exactly twenty-three interments. At this stage the Burgermeister saw himself in a position to inform the Grand Duke and Goethe of his search and its success. From both he received grateful acknowledgments. Goethe unhesitatingly recognised the head, and laid stress on the peculiar beauty and evenness of the teeth.

"The new cemetery lay on a gently rising ground on the south side of the town. Schwabe's favourite plan was to deposit what he had found - all that he now ever dreamed of finding - of his beloved poet on the highest point of the slope, and to mark the spot by a simple monument, so that travellers at their first approach might know where the head of Schiller lay. One forenoon in early spring he led Frau von Wolzogen and the Chancellor von Muller to the spot. They approved his plan, and the remaining members of Schiller's family - all of whom had left Weimar - signified their assent. They 'did not desire,' as one of themselves expressed it, 'to strive against Nature's appointment that man's earthly remains should be reunited with herself;' they would prefer that their father's dust should rest in the ground rather than anywhere else. But the Grand Duke and Goethe decided otherwise.

"Dannecker's colossal bust of Schiller had recently been acquired for the Grand Ducal library, where it had been placed on a lofty pedestal opposite the bust of Goethe; and in this pedestal, which was hollow, it was resolved to deposit the skull. The consent of the family having been obtained, the solemnity was delayed till the arrival of Ernst von Schiller, who could not reach Weimar before autumn. On September the 17th the ceremony took place. A few persons had been invited, amongst whom, of course, was the Burgermeister. Goethe, more suo, dreaded the agitation and remained at home, but sent his son to represent him as chief librarian. A cantata having been sung, Ernst von Schiller, in a short speech, thanked all persons present, but especially the Burgermeister, for the love they had

C. M. Ingleby

shown to the memory of his father. He then formally delivered his father's head into the hands of the younger Goethe, who, reverently receiving it, thanked his friend in Goethe's name, and having dwelt on the affection that had subsisted between their fathers vowed that the precious relic should thenceforward be guarded with anxious care. Up to this moment the skull had been wrapped in a cloth and sealed: the younger Goethe now made it over to the librarian, Professor Riemer, to be unpacked and placed in its receptacle. All present subscribed their names, the pedestal was locked, and the key carried home to Goethe.

"None doubted that Schiller's head was now at rest for many years. But it had already occurred to Goethe, who had more osteological knowledge than the excellent Burgermeister, that, the skull being in their possession, it would be possible to find the skeleton. A very few days after the ceremony in the library, he sent to Jena, begging the Professor of Anatomy, Dr. Schroter, to have the kindness to spend a day or two at Weimar, and to bring with him, if possible, a functionary of the Jena Museum, Farber by name, who had at one time been Schiller's servant. As soon as they arrived, Goethe placed the matter in Schroter's hands. Again the head was raised from its pillow and carried back to the dismal Kasselgewolbe, where the bones still lay in a heap. The chief difficulty was to find the first vertebra; after that all was easy enough. With some exceptions, comparatively trifling, Schroter succeeded in reproducing the skeleton, which then was laid in a new coffin 'lined with blue merino,' and would seem (though we are not distinctly told) to have been deposited in the library. Professor Schroter's register of bones recovered and bones missing has been both preserved and printed. The skull was restored to its place in the pedestal. There was another shriek from the public at these repeated violations of the tomb; and the odd position chosen for Schiller's head, apart from his body, called forth, not without reason, abundant criticism.

"Schwabe's idea of a monument in the new cemetery was, after a while, revived by the Grand Duke, Carl August, but with an important alteration, which was, that on the spot indicated at the head of the rising ground there should be erected a common sepulchre for Goethe and Schiller, in which the latter's remains should at once be deposited - the mausoleum to be finally closed only when, in the course of nature, Goethe should have been laid there too. The idea was, doubtless, very noble, and found great favour with Goethe himself, who entering into it commissioned Coudray, the architect, to sketch the plan of a simple mausoleum, in which the sarcophagi were to be visible from without. There was some delay in clearing the ground - a nursery of young trees had to be removed - so that at Midsummer, 1827, nothing had been done. It is said that the intrigues of certain persons, who made a point of opposing Goethe at all times, prevailed so far with the Grand Duke that he became indifferent about the whole scheme. Meanwhile it was necessary to provide for the remains of Schiller. The public voice was loud in condemning their present location, and in August, 1827, Louis of Bavaria again appeared as a Deus ex machina to hasten on the last act. He expressed surprise that the bones of Germany's best-beloved should be kept like rare coins, or other curiosities, in a public museum. In these circum-stances, the Grand Duke wrote Goethe a note, proposing for his approval that the skull and skeleton of Schiller should be reunited and 'provisionally'

C. M. Ingleby

deposited in the vault which the Grand Duke had built for himself and his house, 'until Schiller's family should otherwise determine.' No better plan seeming feasible, Goethe himself gave orders for the construction of a sarcophagus. On November 17th, 1827, in presence of the younger Goethe, Coudray and Riemer, the head was finally removed from the pedestal, and Professor Schroter reconstructed the entire skeleton in this new and more sumptuous abode, which we are told was seven feet in length, and bore at its upper end the name SCHILLER

in letters of cast-iron. That same afternoon Goethe went himself to the library and expressed his satisfaction with all that had been done.

At last, on December 16th, 1827, at half-past five in the morning, a few persons again met at the same place. The Grand Duke had desired - for what reason we know not - to avoid observation; it was Schiller's fate that his remains should be carried hither and hither by stealth and in the night. Some tapers burned around the bier: the recesses of the hall were in darkness. Not a word was spoken, but those present bent for an instant in silent prayer, on which the bearers raised the coffin and carried it away. They walked along through the park: the night was cold and cloudy: some of the party had lanterns. When they reached the avenue that led up to the cemetery, the moon shone out as she had done twenty-two years before. At the vault itself some other friends had assembled, amongst whom was the Mayor. Ere the lid was finally secured, Schwabe placed himself at the head of the coffin, and recognised the skull to be that which he had rescued from the Kassengewolbe. The sarcophagus having then been closed, and a laurel wreath laid on it, formal possession, in the name of the Grand Duke, was taken by the Marshal, Freiherr von Spiegel. The key was removed to be kept in possession of his Excellency, the Geheimrath von Goethe, as head of the Institutions for Art and Science. This key, in an envelope, addressed by Goethe, is said to be preserved in the Grand Ducal Library, where, however, we have no recollection of having seen it.

The 'provisional' deposition has proved more permanent than any other. Whoever would see the resting-place of Goethe and Schiller must descend into the Grand Ducal vault, where, through a grating, in the twilight beyond he will catch a glimpse of their sarcophagi."

The other case of exhumation, and reinterment with funeral rites, which I deem of sufficient importance to be recorded here, is that of the great Raphael. In this the motive was not, as in that of Schiller, to give his bones a worthier resting-place, nor yet, as in so many other cases, to gratify a morbid curiosity, but to set at rest a question of disputed identity. In this respect the case of Raphael has a special bearing upon the matter in hand. I extract the following from Mrs. Jameson's Lives of Italian Painters, ed. 1874, p. 258:

"In the year 1833 there arose among the antiquarians of Rome a keen dispute concerning a human skull, which on no evidence whatever, except a long-received tradition, had been preserved and exhibited in the Academy of St. Luke as the skull of Raphael. Some even expressed a doubt as to the exact place of his sepulchre, though upon this point the contemporary testimony seemed to leave no room for uncertainty.

C. M. Ingleby

"To ascertain the fact, permission was obtained from the Papal Government, and from the canons of the Church of the Rotunda (i.e., of the Pantheon), to make some researches; and on the 14th of September in the same year, after five days spent in removing the pavement in several places, the remains of Raphael were discovered in a vault behind the high altar, and certified as his by indisputable proofs. After being examined, and a cast made from the skull and [one] from the right hand, the skeleton was exhibited publicly in a glass case, and multitudes thronged to the church to look upon it. On the 18th of October, 1833, a second funeral ceremony took place. The remains were deposited in a pine-wood coffin, then in a marble sarcophagus, presented by the Pope (Gregory XVI), and reverently consigned to their former resting-place, in presence of more than three thousand spectators, including almost all the artists, the officers of government, and other persons of the highest rank in Rome."

This event, as will appear in the sequel, is our best precedent for not permitting a sentimental respect for departed greatness to interfere with the respectful examination of a great man's remains, wherever such examination may determine a question to which "universal history is NOT indifferent."

Toland tells us that Milton's body was, on November 12, 1674, carried "to the Church of S. Giles, near Cripplegate, where he lies buried in the Chancel; and where the Piety of his Admirers will shortly erect a Monument becoming his worth, and the incouragement of Letters in King William's Reign." {19} It appears that his body was laid next to that of his father. A plain stone only was placed over the spot; and this, if

Aubrey's account be trustworthy, was removed in 1679, when the two steps were raised which lead to the altar. The remains, however, were undisturbed for nearly sixteen years. On the 4th of August, 1790, according to a small volume written by Philip Neve, Esq. (of which two editions were published in the same year), Milton's coffin was removed, and his remains exhibited to the public on the 4th and 5th of that month. Mr. George Steevens, the great editor of Shakespeare, who justly denounced the indignity INTENDED, not offered, to the great Puritan poet's remains by Royalist landsharks, satisfied himself that the corpse was that of a woman of fewer years than Milton. Thus did good Providence, or good fortune, defeat the better half of their nefarious project: and I doubt not their gains were spent as money is which has been "gotten over the devil's back." Steevens' assurance gives us good reason for believing that Mr. Philip Neve's indignant protest is only good in the general, and that Milton's "hallowed reliques" still "rest undisturb'd within their peaceful shrine." I have adduced this instance to serve as an example of what I condemn, and should, in any actual case, denounce as strongly as Mr. Philip Neve or George Steevens. To expose a man's remains after any interval for the purpose of treating his memory with indignity, or of denouncing an unpopular cause which he espoused, or (worst of all) "to fine his bones," or make money by the public exhibition of his dust, deserves unmeasured and unqualified reprobation, and every prudent measure should be taken to render such an act impossible.

To take another example of the reprehensible practice of despoiling the grave of a great enemy: Oliver Cromwell was, as is proved by the most reliable evidence, namely, that of a trustworthy eye-witness, buried on the scene of his greatest achievement, the Field of Naseby. Some Royalist Philister is said to have discovered, and stolen from its resting-place, the embalmed head of the great Protector. It found its way to London towards the end of the last century, where it was exhibited at No. 5, Mead Court, Old Bond Street. {20} It is said to have been acquired by Sir Joshua Reynolds in September, 1786, and to be now or late in the collection of Mr. W. A. Wilkinson, of Beckenham. It is recorded in one of the Additional Manuscripts in the British Museum, under date April 21, 1813, that "an offer was made this morning to bring it to Soho Square, to show it to Sir Joseph Banks, but he desired to be excused from seeing THE REMAINS OF THE OLD VILLANOUS REPUBLICAN, THE MENTION OF WHOSE VERY NAME MAKES HIS BLOOD BOIL WITH INDIGNATION. The same offer was made to Sir Joseph forty years ago, which he also refused." What a charming specimen was Banks of the genus Tory! But after all it is a comfort to think that on this occasion he was right: for while this head was undoubtedly that which did duty for the Protector at Tyburn, and was afterwards fixed on the top of Westminster Hall, it was almost certainly not that of Oliver Cromwell: whose remains probably still lie crumbling into dust in their unknown grave on Naseby Field. {21a}

I give one more example of robbing the grave of an illustrious man, through the superstition of many and the cupidity of one. Swedenborg was buried in the vault of the Swedish Church in Prince's Square, on April 5, 1772. In 1790, in order to determine a question raised in debate, viz., whether Swedenborg were really dead and buried, his wooden coffin was opened, and the leaden one was sawn across the breast. A few days after, a party of Swedenborgians visited the vault. "Various relics" (says White: Life of Swedenborg, 2nd ed., 1868, p. 675) "were carried off: Dr. Spurgin told me he possessed the cartilage of an ear. Exposed to the air, the flesh quickly fell to dust, and a skeleton was all that remained for subsequent visitors. {21b} At a funeral in 1817, Granholm, an officer in the Swedish Navy, seeing the lid of Swedenborg's coffin loose, abstracted the skull, and hawked it about amongst London Swedenborgians, but none would buy. Dr. Wahlin, pastor of the Swedish Church, recovered what he supposed to be the stolen skull, had a cast of it taken, and placed it in the coffin in 1819. The cast which is sometimes seen in phrenological collections is obviously not Swedenborg's: it is thought to be that of a small female skull."

In the latter part of the reign of George III a mausoleum was built in the Tomb House at Windsor Castle. On its completion, in the spring of 1813, it was determined to open a passage of communication with St. George's Chapel, and in constructing this an opening was accidentally made in one of the walls of the vault of Henry VIII, through which the workmen could see three coffins, one of which was covered with a black velvet pall. It was known that Henry VIII and Queen Jane Seymour were buried in this vault, but a question had been raised as to the place of Charles the First's interment, through the statement of Lord Clarendon, that the search made for the late King's coffin at Windsor (with a view to its removal to Westminster Abbey) had proved fruitless. Sir Henry Halford, in his Account, appended to his Essays and Orations, 1831, {22} thus describes the examination of the palled coffin.

"On representing the circumstance to the Prince Regent, his R. H. perceived at once that A DOUBTFUL POINT IN HISTORY MIGHT BE CLEARED UP BY OPENING THIS VAULT; and accordingly his R. H. ordered an examination to be made on the first convenient opportunity. This was done on the First of April last [i.e., 1813], the day after the funeral of the Duchess of Brunswick, in the presence of his R. H. himself, who guaranteed thereby THE MOST RESPECTFUL CARE AND ATTENTION TO THE REMAINS OF THE DEAD, during the enquiry. His R. H. was accompanied by his R. H. the Duke of Cumberland, Count Munster, the Dean of Windsor, Benjamin Charles Stevenson, Esq., and Sir Henry Halford."

"The vault was accordingly further opened and explored, and the palled coffin, which was of lead, and bore the inscription 'King Charles, 1648,' was opened at the head. A second Charles I, coffin of wood was thus disclosed, and, through this, the body carefully wrapped up in cere-cloth, into the folds of which a quantity of unctuous or greasy matter, mixed with resin, as it seemed, had been melted, so as to exclude, as effectually as possible, the external air. The coffin was completely full; and, from the tenacity of the cere-cloth, great difficulty was experienced in detaching it successfully from the parts which it enveloped. Wherever the unctuous matter had insinuated itself, the separation of the cere-cloth was easy; and when it came off, a correct impression of the features to which it had been applied was observed in the unctuous substance. {23} At length the whole face was disengaged from its covering. The complexion of the skin was dark and discoloured. The forehead and temples had lost little or nothing of their muscular substance; the cartilage of the nose was gone; but the left eye, in the first moment of exposure, was open and full, though it vanished almost immediately: and the pointed beard, so characteristic of the reign of King Charles, was perfect. The shape of the face was a long oval; many of the teeth remained; and the left ear, in consequence of the interposition of the unctuous matter between it and the cere-cloth, was found entire."

The head was found to be loose, and was once more held up to view; and after a careful examination of it had been made, and a sketch taken, and the identity fully established, it was immediately replaced in the coffin, which was soldered up and restored to the vault. Of the other two coffins, the larger one had been battered in about the middle, and the skeleton of Henry VIII, exhibiting some beard upon the chin, was exposed to view. The other coffin was left, as it was found, intact. Neither of these coffins bore any inscription.

In the Appendix to Allan Cunningham's Life of Burns {24} we read of an examination of the poet's Tomb, made immediately after that life was published:

"When Burns' Mausoleum was opened in March, 1834, to receive the remains of his widow, some residents in Dumfries obtained the consent of her nearest relative to take a cast from the cranium of the poet. This was done during the night between the 31st March and 1st April. Mr. Archibald Blacklock, surgeon, drew up the following description:

"The cranial bones were perfect in every respect, if we except a little erosion of their external table, and firmly held together by their sutures, &c., &c. Having completed our intention [i.e., of taking a plaster cast of the skull, washed from every particle of sand, &c.], the skull, securely closed in a leaden case, was again committed to the earth, precisely where we found it. - Archd. Blacklock.'"

The last example I shall adduce is that of Ben Jonson's skull. On this Lieut.-Colonel Cunningham thus writes:

"In my boyhood I was familiar with the Abbey, and well remember the 'pavement square of blew marble, 14 inches square, with O Rare Ben Jonson,' which marked the poet's grave. When Buckland was Dean, the spot had to be disturbed for the coffin of Sir Robert Wilson, and the Dean sent his son Frank, now so well known as an agreeable writer on Natural History, to see whether he could observe anything to confirm, or otherwise, the tradition about Jonson being buried in a standing posture. The workmen, he tells us, 'found a coffin very much decayed, which from the appearance of the remains must have originally been placed in the upright position. The skull found among these remains, Spice, the gravedigger, gave me as that of Ben Jonson, and I took it at once into the Dean's study. We examined it together, and then going into the Abbey carefully returned it to the earth.' In 1859, when John Hunter's coffin was removed to the Abbey, the same spot had to be dug up, and Mr. Frank Buckland again secured the skull of Jonson, placing it at the last moment on the coffin of the great surgeon. So far, so good; but not long afterwards, a statement appeared in the 'Times' that the skull of Ben Jonson was in the possession of a blind gentleman at Stratford-upon-Avon. Hereupon Mr. Buckland made further inquiries, and calmly tells us that he has convinced himself that the skull which he had taken such care of on two occasions, [such care as not so much as to measure or sketch it!] was not Jonson's skull at all; that a Mr. Ryde had anticipated him both times in removing and replacing the genuine article, [!] and that the Warwickshire claimant [!] was a third skull which Mr. Ryde observed had been purloined from the grave on the second opening. Mr. Buckland is a scientific naturalist, and an ardent worshipper of the closest of all observers, John Hunter. Now mark what satisfies such a man on such an occasion as this. He was wrong and Mr. Ryde was right, because Mr. Ryde described HIS skull as having RED HAIR; and in Aubrey's Lives of Eminent Men, 'I find evidence quite sufficient for any medical man to come to the conclusion that Ben Jonson's hair was in all probability of a red colour, though the fact IS NOT STATED IN SO MANY WORDS.' In so many words! I think not! Actually all that Aubrey says on the subject is, 'HE WAS, OR RATHER HAD BEEN, OF A CLEARE AND FAIRE SKIN'! (Lives, ii, 414.) And this, too, in spite of our knowing from his own pen, and from more than one painting, that his hair was as black as the raven's wing! Besides, he was sixty-five years old when he died, and we may be sure that the few locks he had left were neither red nor black, but of the hue of the 'hundred of grey hairs' which he described as remaining eighteen years before. Mr. Buckland's statement will be found in the Fourth Series of his Curiosities of Natural History, one of the most entertaining little volumes with which we are acquainted." {26}

In reviewing the various incidents connected with the foregoing cases of exhumation one is perhaps most struck with the last two. That an illustrious man of science, and his son, who at that time must already have been a scientific naturalist, should have cooperated in so stupendous a blunder as the mere inspection of Ben Jonson's skull, without taking so much as a measurement or drawing of it, would be incredible, but for the fact that both are dead, and nothing of the sort has come to light: and it is scarcely less surprising that the Swedenborgians, who believed themselves to be in possession of their founder's skull, should not have left on record some facts concerning its shape and size.

Before addressing myself to the principal matter of this essay, namely the question whether we should not attempt to recover Shakespeare's skull, I may as well note, that the remains of the great philosopher, whom so many regard as Shakespeare's very self, or else his alter ego, were not allowed to remain unmolested in their grave in St. Michael's Church, St. Albans. Thomas Fuller, in his Worthies, relates as follows: "Since I have read that his grave being occasionally opened [!] his scull (the relique of civil veneration) was by one King, a Doctor of Physick, made the object of scorn and contempt; but he who then derided the dead has since become the laughingstock of the living." This, being quoted by a correspondent in Notes and Queries {27a} elicited from Mr. C. Le Poer Kennedy, of St. Albans, {27b} an account of a search that had been made for Bacon's remains, on the occasion of the interment of the last Lord Verulam. "A partition wall was pulled down, and the search extended into the part of the vault immediately under the monument, but no remains were found." On the other hand, we have the record of his express wish to be buried there. I am afraid the doctor, who is said to have become the laughingstock of the living, has entirely faded out of men's minds and memories.

Among the many protests against the act of exhumation, I select that of Capel Lofft, as representative of the rest. He writes - "It were to be wished that neither superstition, affectation, idle curiosity, or avarice, were so frequently invading the silence of the grave. Far from dishonouring the illustrious dead, it is rather outraging the common condition of humanity, and last melancholy state in which our present existence terminates. Dust and ashes have no intelligence to give, whether beauty, genius, or virtue, informed the animated clay. A tooth of Homer or Milton will not be distinguished from one of a common mortal; nor a bone of Alexander acquaint us with more of his character than one of Bucephalus. Though the dead be unconcerned, the living are neither benefited nor improved: decency is violated, and a kind of instinctive sympathy infringed, which, though it ought not to overpower reason, ought not without it, and to no purpose, to be superseded." Notwithstanding the right feeling shewn in this passage, it is quite sufficient to condemn Capel Lofft as a Philister. Let us for a moment examine some of these very eloquent assertions. Agreeing as I cordially do with his wish, that neither superstition, affectation, whatever that may mean, idle curiosity, or avarice, were the motives which actuate those who molest the relics of the dead, I cannot allow that neither dust and ashes, bones, nor teeth, have any intelligence to give us; nor yet that by the reverential scrutiny of those relics the living can be neither benefited nor improved. All that depends upon the intelligence of the scrutineer. Doubtless your Philister would turn over the skull or the bones, or make hay with the dust, just as Peter Bell could see nothing in a primrose but a weed in flower. What message a bone or a weed may have for the man or the race depends wholly upon the recipient. Your

Shakespeare or Goethe, your Owen or Huxley, would find in it an intelligible language; while your Capel Lofft would denounce what he found there as dirt and indecency. How true is the proverb of Syr Oracle Martext: "To the wise all things are wise." In the case of Schiller, the skull spoke for itself, and claimed to be that of Schiller; the bones, like those in the 37th chapter of Ezekiel, aggregated themselves around their head, and submitted to an accurate articulation; and the teeth gave their evidence, too, at least the place of one, which was not in the jaw, bore its testimony to the fact that the jaw in question was that which Schiller had submitted to dentistry. In the case of Raphael, the discovery of the skull disproved the claims of the spurious relic, and arrested a stupid superstition. {29} Beyond question, the skull of Shakespeare, might we but discover it in anything like its condition at the time of its interment, would be of still greater interest and value. It would at least settle two disputed points in the Stratford Bust; it would test the Droeshout print, and every one of the half-dozen portraits-in-oils which pass as presentments of Shakespeare's face at different periods of his life. Moreover it would pronounce decisively on the pretensions of the Kesselstadt Death-Mask, and we should know whether that was from the "flying-mould" after which Gerard Johnson worked, when he sculptured the Bust. Negative evidence the skull would assuredly furnish; but there is reason for believing that it would afford positive evidence in favour of the Bust, one or other of the portraits, or even of the Death-Mask: and why, I ask, should not an attempt be made to recover Shakespeare's skull? Why should not the authorities of Stratford, to whom this brochure is inscribed, sanction, or even themselves undertake, a respectful examination of the grave in which Shakespeare's remains are believed to have been buried?

Two grounds have always been assigned for abstention: (1) the sentiment which disposes men to leave the relics of the dead to their rest in the tomb: (2) the prohibition contained in the four lines inscribed upon Shakespeare's gravestone. With the former of these I have sufficiently dealt already. As for the latter; the prohibitory lines, whether they proceeded from our Poet himself, as Mr. William Page, and many before him, believed, or from the pen of Ben Jonson, or of an inferior writer (which is to me the more probable authorship), I am most desirous to respect them; not that I stand in awe of Shakespeare's curse, but because I think they proceeded from a natural and laudable fear. I have no more doubt that "moves," in the quatrain, means "REmoves," than I have that "stones" means "GRAVEstones." The fear which dictated these curious lines, was, I believe, lest Shakespeare's remains should be carried, whither so many of his predecessors in the churchyard had been carried, to the common charnel-house hard-by. I do not read in those lines a prohibition against an examination of the grave, say for purposes of knowledge and history, but against the despoiling of that grave, to make room for some local knight, squire, or squireen, who might have been deemed a worthier tenant of the Chancel room. Shakespeare's body was carried to the grave on Thursday, April 25, 1616 (O. S.); and, beyond question, his son-in-law, Dr. John Hall, made all the arrangements, and bore all the expenses. We have no proof whatever that the grave has remained closed from that time: on the contrary there is some slight scintilla of proof that it has been explored; and it would never astonish me to learn that Shakespeare's skull had been abstracted! There may yet be some among us who have a personal interest in preventing such an exploration, and in thus maintaining the general belief, that Shakespeare's relics still rest in the mould in which they were buried.

Be that as it may: in the year 1796, the supposed grave was actually broken into, in the course of digging a vault in its immediate proximity; and not much more than fifty years ago the slab over the grave, having sunk below the level of the pavement, was removed, the surface was levelled, and a fresh stone was laid over the old bed. It is certain, I believe, that the original stone did not bear the name of Shakespeare, any more than its successor: but it is not certain that the four lines appear upon the new stone in exactly the same literal form as they did upon the old one. {31} I wish I could add that these two were the only occasions when either grave or gravestone was meddled with. I am informed, on the authority of a Free and Accepted Mason, that a Brother-Mason of his has explored the grave which purports to be Shakespeare's, and that he found nothing in it but dust. The former statement must be taken cum grano. Granting this, however, the latter statement will not surprise my valued friend Mr. J. O. Halliwell-Phillipps, who thinks he sees a reason for the disappearance of Shakespeare's Bones, in the fact that his coffin was buried in the Chancel mould. {32} If this be all the ground of his assurance, that nothing but dust would reward the search, I would say "despair thy charm;" for many corpses so buried have for many years been preserved in comparative freshness - corpses which had been treated with no more care than the body of Shakespeare is believed to have received. The last case to come to my knowledge, was that of the Birmingham poet, John Freeth, the father of my old friend John

Freeth, formerly the Clerk (or principal manager) of the Birmingham Canal Navigations. On the destruction of the burial-place of the Old Meeting House, in Old Meeting Street, Birmingham, in March, 1882, the coffin of the poet was found in the earth, and on opening it, the face was almost as fresh, and quite as perfect, as on the day of the old man's interment seventy-four years before: and as to his bones? Does Mr. Halliwell-Phillipps believe that in a period but little more than double that of the poet Freeth's unmolested repose, namely 180 years, all Shakespeare's Bones would have been turned to dust, and become indistinguishable from the mould in which the coffin lay? To ask this question is to answer it. A more credulous man, than I know Mr. Halliwell-Phillipps to be, would hesitate to give an affirmative answer. Depend upon it, Shakespeare's skull is in his grave, unchanged; or it has been abstracted. There may well have been a mistake as to the exact locality of the grave: for we do not know that the new gravestone was laid down exactly over the place of the one that was removed; and the skull may be found in a grave hard-by. But if, on making a thorough search, no skull be found, I shall believe that it has been stolen: for, apart from the fact of its non-discovery, I should almost be disposed to say, that no superstition, or fear of Shakespeare's curse, nor any official precaution and vigilance, could have been a match for that combination of curiosity, cupidity, and relic-worship, which has so often prompted and carried out the exhumation of a great man's bones. If there were no other reason for searching Shakespeare's grave, save the extinction of an unpleasant but not irrational doubt, I would forthwith perform the exploration, and if possible obtain tangible proof that the poet's skull had not been removed from its resting-place.

C. M. Ingleby

But the exploration, if successful, would have a bearing upon more material issues. The most opposite judgments have been passed upon the Bust, both as a work of art and as a copy of nature. Landor, whose experience of Italian art was considerable, recorded it as his opinion, that it was the noblest head ever sculptured; while Mr. Hain Friswell depreciated it, declaring it to be "rudely cut and heavy, without any feeling, a mere block": smooth and round like a boy's marble. {33} After some of Mr. Friswell's deliverances, I am not disposed to rank his judgment very high; and I accept Lander's decision. As to the finish of the face, Mr. Fairholt's criticism is an exaggeration, successfully exposed by Mr. Friswell. My own opinion, telle quelle, has been already printed. {34} Allowing the bust to have been a recognisable, if not a staring likeness of the poet, I said and still say - "How awkward is the ensemble of the face! What a painful stare, with its goggle eyes and gaping mouth! The expression of this face has been credited with humour, bonhommie and jollity. To me it is decidedly clownish; and is suggestive of a man crunching a sour apple, or struck with amazement at some unpleasant spectacle. Yet there is force in the lineaments of this muscular face." The large photograph of the Monument lately issued by the New Shakspere Society, as well as those more successful issues of Mr. Thrupp's studio, fully bears out this judgment. But the HEAD, as Landor said, is noble. Without accepting the suggestion that the sculptor had met with an accident to the nose, and had, in consequence, to lengthen the upper lip, I think it self-evident that there is some little derangement of natural proportions in those features; the nose, especially, being ill-formed and undersized for the rest of the face. If we had but Shakespeare's skull before us, most of these questions would be set at rest for ever.

Among the relics once religiously preserved in the Kesselstadt collection at Mayence was a plaster mask, having at the back the year of Shakespeare's death. This relic had been in that collection time out of mind, and seems always to have been received as a cast from the "flying-mould" of Shakespeare's dead face. With this was a small oil-painting of a man crowned with bays, lying on a state bier; of which, by the kindness of Mr. J. Parker Norris of Philadelphia, I am able to give the admirable engraving which forms the frontispiece to this little volume. On the death of Count and Canon Francis von Kesselstadt, at Mayence, in 1843, the family museum was broken up, and its contents dispersed. No more was seen or heard of either of the two relics described, till 1847, when the painting was purchased by an artist named Ludwig Becker; and after some months of unremitting search he discovered the Death-Mask in a broker's shop, and this he bought in 1849. The purchaser is dead: but both these relics are in the Grand Ducal Museum at Darmstadt, and belong to its curator, Dr. Ernst Becker, Ludwig's brother. I have inspected both with the keenest interest; and I am of opinion that the painting is not after the mask. The date, 1637, which it bears, led Dr. Schaafhausen to think that it was intended for Ben Jonson; a view to some extent borne out by the portrait of Ben in the Dulwich Gallery. {35} By others, however, it is believed to be a fancy portrait of Shakespeare, based upon the Death-Mask. Now the Bust was believed to have been sculptured after a death-mask. Is the Becker Mask that from which Gerard Johnson worked? If so, there must have been a fatal accident indeed to the nose; for the nose of the mask is a long and finely arched one: the upper lip is shorter than that of the bust, and the forehead is more receding.

Of the many alleged portraits of Shakespeare there are but two whose pedigree stretches back into the seventeenth century, and is lost in obscurity there. The origin of the vast majority of the claimants is only too well known, or shrewdly suspected: these are (1) copies, more or less unfaithful, of older pictures; (2) idealised portraits, based upon such older ones, or upon the Bust; (3) genuine portraits of unknown persons, valued for some slight or imaginary resemblance to the Bust, or to such older portraits, or for having passed as Shakespeare's, and thus offering the means of selling dear what had been bought cheap; (4) impostures. As I am not writing an essay upon the portraits, I will merely mention in the order of their importance the few claimants whose title merits the least consideration.

I. - The Droeshout engraving, prefixed to the first collective edition of the Poet's works, published in 1623: i.e., the print in its early state.

II. - The so-called Janssen portrait (on wood) in the collection of the Duke of Somerset. This has been traced back to 1761, when it was purchased by Charles Jennens, Esq., of Gopsall. Its identity with the portrait which was purchased for the Duke of Hamilton and Brandon in 1809 is, at least, highly probable. In 1811 Woodburn published the first engraving from it, and stated that the picture had belonged to Prince Rupert, who left it to Mrs. E. S. Howes on his death in 1682. No actual proof of this was given, nor did Woodburn mention Jennens' ownership.

III. - The Croker portrait. We have it on the authority

of Boaden that this portrait, which he said was the property of the Right Hon. J. Wilson Croker, was a replica of the Janssen. There was a mystery, not in the least cleared up, concerning these two pictures and their history. I am unable to ascertain who at present owns the later one. Collectors of the prints can always distinguish between the two. The only engraving of the Croker portrait was by R. Cooper; published January 1, 1824, by G. Smeeton, and is an oval in a shaded rectangle. All the rest are either from the Janssen, or from Dunkarton's engraving of it. {37}

IV. - The Chandos portrait (on wood) in the National Portrait Gallery at South Kensington. It has been traced back to 1668, when, on Davenant's death, it passed to John Otway: but not in its present or even late condition.

V. - The Lumley portrait, well known through the admirable chromo-lithograph, by Mr. Vincent Brooks (which is scarcely distinguishable from the original), and once sold for forty guineas as the original portrait. It has been traced back to 1785.

VI. - The Ashbourne portrait.

VII. - The Felton portrait (on wood), traced back to 1792.

VIII. - The Challis portrait (on wood).

IX. - The Hunt portrait: at the Birthplace. This is not in its original state, and cannot be judged-of apart from a copy of it in the possession of John Rabone, Esq., of Birmingham.

C. M. Ingleby

Of these III, VI, and VIII have not been satisfactorily traced back even into the last century.

Beyond question, after the Bust and the Droeshout engraving, the Janssen portrait has the greatest value. Unfortunately the Chandos, even if its history be as stated, is of very little real value: for it has been so often repaired or "restored," and is at present in such a dilapidated condition, that it cannot be relied upon as a portrait. Moreover it bears but little resemblance to the admirable drawing from it in its former state, made by Ozias Humphreys in the year 1783. This drawing is an exceedingly fine work of art, to which even Scriven's print, good as it is, scarcely does justice. To compare Humphreys' drawing, which hangs in the Birthplace, and is its most valuable portrait, with Samuel Cousin's fine mezzotint of the Chandos, engraved forty years ago, is to be convinced that the existing picture no longer represents the man - whosoever he may have been - from whom it was painted. How many questions, affecting the Bust, the Death-Mask, and these portraits, would be set at rest by the production of Shakespeare's skull!

The late Mr. William Page, the American sculptor, whose interest in testing the identity of the Kesselstadt Death-Mask, by comparing it with Shakespeare's skull, was in 1874-5 incomparably greater than that of any other interested person, comes VERY NEAR the expression of a wish for the exhumation of the skull. {39} But he had not the courage to express that wish, and after the passage which I am about to quote, abruptly changes the subject. He says, "The man who wrote the four lines [of epitaph] which have thus far secured his bones that rest which his epitaph demands, omitted nothing likely to carry the whole plan into effect. The authorship of the epitaph cannot be doubted, unless another man in England had the wit and wisdom to divine the loyal heart's core of its people, and touch it in the single appeal 'for Jesus sake.' Nothing else has kept him out of Westminster [Abbey]. The style of the command and curse are Shakespearian, and triumphant as any art of forethought in his plays." Then follows on - without even the break of a paragraph - not what naturally should have followed, and MUST have been in Mr. Page's mind, but a citation of Chantrey and John Bell, as to the model from which the Bust was made. Possibly it is due to the omission of a sentence, which once intervened between the remarks on the remains and those which concern the Bust of Shakespeare, that we have now two totally different matters in juxtaposition, and in the same paragraph. In this Death-Mask Mr. Page saw the reconciliation of the Bust, the Droeshout print (in its best state), and the Chandos portrait. I do not meddle with that opinion, or the evidences upon which it rests. But I have inspected all the four: I have also seen Mr. Page's life-size bronze bust, and wish I had never seen it, or even a photograph of it, for it destroyed for me a pleasant dream.

But whatever be the value of Mr. Page's conclusion, or of his Bust, I have no doubt that the value of his book lies in those accurate "Dimensions of Shakespeare's Mask," which he took during his six days of free access to the Grand Ducal Museum. The measurements are on pp. 51-55 of his book, and may eventually be of the greatest possible use, if the time should ever arrive when Shakespeare's skull will be subjected to similar measurement. For myself, I am disposed to believe that no mistaken sense of duty on the part of the Stratford authorities will long be able to prevent that examination, if the skull be still in existence.

A BIBLIOGRAPHY OF THE EXHUMATION QUESTION AS AFFECTING SHAKESPEARE'S BONES.

1. - Hawthorne, Nathaniel, in "Recollections of a Gifted Woman," in Our Old Home (reprinted from the Atlantic Monthly, January, 1863), records Miss Delia Bacon's project for exploring Shakespeare's grave, and the failure of her attempt through the irresolution occasioned by her fear of disappointment.

2. - Norris, J. Parker, in the New York American Bibliopolist, of April, 1876, vol. viii, p. 38, in the section entitled "Shakspearian Gossip" [reprinted in the Philadelphia Press, August 4, 1876], seriously proposes the exhumation of Shakespeare's remains, and asks, "Is it not worth making an effort to secure 'the counterfeit presentment' of him who wrote 'for all time'? If we could even get a photograph of Shakspeare's skull it would be a great thing, and would help us to make a better portrait of him than we now possess." His courageous article is particularly useful for the adduction of cases in which corpses have lain in the grave far longer than that of Shakespeare, and been discovered in a state of comparative perfection. What would one not give to look upon Shakespeare's dead face!

The letter of " a friend residing near Stratford," from

C. M. Ingleby

which he gives a long extract, was from one of my present colleagues in the Shakespeare Trust, viz.:

3. - Timmins, Sam., as quoted in the last recorded article, writes - "Some graves of the Shakspeare date were opened at Church Lawford a few years ago, and the figures, faces, and dresses were perfect, but, of course, in half an hour were mere heaps of dust. Shakspeare's grave is near the Avon, but doubtless he was buried well (in a leaden coffin probably), and there is scarcely room for a doubt that, with proper precautions, photographs of his face might be taken perfectly. Surely the end does justify the means here. It is not to satisfy mere idle curiosity. It is not mere relic-mongering; it is simply to secure for posterity what we could give - an exact representation of the great poet as he lived and died. Surely this is justifiable, at least it is allowable, in the absence of any authentic portrait. Surely such a duty might be most reverently done. I doubt after all if it will be; but I am very strongly in favour of the trial, and if no remains were found, no harm would be done, the 'curse' to the contrary notwithstanding. People who have pet projects about portraits would not like to have all their neat and logical arguments knocked on the head, but where SHOULD we ALL be if no Shakspeare at all were found, but only a bundle of musty old MSS. in Lord Bacon's 'fine Roman hand'? After all, I am rather nervous about the result of such an exhumation. But, seriously, I see no reason why it should not be made. A legal friend here long ago suggested (humorously, not professionally of course) that the 'curse' might be escaped by employing a woman ('cursed be HE') and women would compete for the honor!"

4. - Anonymous Article in The Birmingham Daily

Mail, of August 23, 1876, headed "Shakspeare's Carte de Visite." This is strongly adverse to Mr. Norris's proposals. The writer inclines to believe that the "friend residing near Stratford" was "a fiction of the Mrs. Harris type," or "possibly a modest way of evading the praise which would be the meed of the brilliant genius who originated the project": both very random guesses, and, as it turns out, wide of the mark. The article ends thus: "If Moses had been raised in Massachussetts he would have been wanted to take a camera or some business-cards up Sinai." For our part, if we shall be so fortunate as to find Shakespeare alive in his grave, we shall of course raise him, and invite him to cooperate in the business of photographing his own shining face. But we are not so sanguine as to expect that miracle, though almost as great wonders have been done by the power of this magician. But where is the "triple curse" with which, according to this authority, "that gravestone is weighted"? Quite another view of the inscription is given by Lord Ronald Gower, infra.

5. - Anonymous Article in the London Daily Telegraph, of August 24, 1876: also strongly adverse to Mr. Norris.

6. - Schaafhausen, Hermann, in the Jahrbuch, or Annual, of the German Shakespeare Society, vol. x, 1875, asks: "Should we be afraid to rely on this evidence [agreement of Mask with known portraits, &c.], there is an easy way of settling the question. We can dig up Shakespeare's skull, and compare the two. True, this may seem to offend against the letter of the epitaph

'BLESTE BE EY MAN TY SPARES THES STONES,

AND CVRST BE HE TY MOVES MY BONES.'

But there is no desecration in entrusting the noble remains of the poet to the enquiring eye of science; which will but learn something new from them, and place beyond doubt the value of another precious relic of him, and then restore them to the quiet of the grave." - (From the Tr. N. S. S., 1875-76. Appendix v.)

7. - Anonymous Article, in the Birmingham Daily Post of September 29, 1877, headed "General Grant at Stratford-upon-Avon," in the course of which Dr. Collis, the Vicar of the church there, is reported to have made some indignant remarks upon Mr. Parker Norris's article. "Having dilated upon the cool presumption of the author of the letter [article], Dr. Collis continued, that persons proposing such an experiment would have to walk over his prostrate body before they did it; adding that the writer even forgot to say, 'if you please.'" The American party, however, do not appear to have seen the matter from Mr. Collis's point of view.

8. - Anonymous Article, in the Birmingham Town Crier of November, 1877; a skit upon Mr. Collis's foolish speech. Beyond this censure, however, nil de mortuo. It is to be regretted that the worthy Vicar's remains were not buried in the church, so that persons approaching the grave with a laudable purpose might meet the reverend gentleman's views, and "walk over his prostrate body."

9. - Shakespearian, A, in the Birmingham Daily Post of October 10, 1877, writes a sensible letter, taking Mr. Parker Norris's side of the question.

10. - Anonymous Article in the New York Nation, of May 21, 1878, in which we read: "Is it sacrilegious to ask whether it is wholly impossible to verify the supposition that the Stratford bust is from a death-mask? Would not the present age permit a tender and reverential scientific examination of the grave of Shakespeare?"

11. - Anonymous Article in the Atlantic Monthly, of June, 1878, in the section entitled "The Contributors' Club," where it is said - "Since the time seems to have come when a man's expression of his wishes with regard to what is to be done after his death is violently and persistently opposed by all who survive him, is it not a good opportunity to suggest that perhaps respect has been paid for a long enough time to the doggerel over Shakespeare's grave?

GOOD FRIEND FOR IESVS SAKE FORBEARE,
TO DIGG THE DVST ENCLOASED HEARE:
BLESTE BE EY MAN TY SPARES THES STONES,
AND CVRST BE HE TY MOVES MY BONES. {45}

When we consider how little we know of the great poet, and the possibility of finding something more by an examination of his tomb, it seems as if, with proper care, an investigation might be made that would possibly reward the trouble." The writer concludes thus - "Is it not advisable, then, to avoid waiting till it is too late? That is to say, unless, as I may fear, it is too late already."

12. - Warwickshire Man, A, in the Argosy, of Oct., 1879, in an article entitled, "How Shakespeare's Skull

was Stolen." The vraisemblance of this narrative is amazing. But for the poverty of the concluding portion, which is totally out of keeping with the foregoing part, one might almost accept this as a narrative of fact.

13. - Gower, Ronald, in the Antiquary, of August, 1880, vol. ii, p. 63, "The Shakespeare Death-Mask," concludes thus - "But how, may it be asked, can proof ever be had that this mask is actually that of Shakespeare? Indeed it can never be proved unless such an impossibility should occur as that a jury of matrons should undertake to view the opened grave at Stratford; they at any rate would not need to fear the curse that is written above his grave - for it says, 'Cursed be HE (and not SHE), who stirs that sacred dust.'" This is a 'new version' of the time-honoured line. I note too that Lord Ronald reproduces the "legal friend's" joke in Mr. Parker Norris's article. But I do not say he ever saw it.

14. - Halliwell-Phillipps, J. O., in his Outlines of the Life of Shakespeare, 1st edition, 1881, p. 86: 2nd edition, 1882, p. 172: 3rd edition, 1883, p. 233: writes thus -

"The nearest approach to an excavation into the grave of Shakespeare was made in the summer of the year 1796, in digging a vault in the immediate locality, when an opening appeared which was presumed to indicate the commencement of the site of the bard's remains. The most scrupulous care, however, was taken not to disturb the neighbouring earth in the slightest degree, the clerk having been placed there, until the brickwork of the adjoining vault was completed, to prevent any one making an examination. No relics whatever were visible through the small opening that thus presented itself, and as the poet was buried in the ground, not in a vault, the chancel earth, moreover, formerly absorbing a large degree of moisture, the great probability is that dust alone remains. This consideration may tend to discourage an irreverent opinion expressed by some, that it is due to the interests of science to unfold to the world the material abode which formerly held so great an intellect." Mr. Halliwell-Phillipps has more faith in the alleged precaution than I have. Surely a needy clerk, with an itching palm, would be no match for a relic-hunter. May we not here read between the lines, q. d., 'to allow any one to make free with the masonry and explore the sacred dust?'

15. - Anonymous Article in the Birmingham Daily Gazette, of December 17, 1880, headed "Excavations in the Church and Churchyard of Stratford-upon-Avon." This repeats, on the authority of Washington Irving's Sketch Book, the story recorded by Mr. Halliwell-Phillipps. It is an alarmist article, censuring the Vicar's excavations, which were made indeed with a laudable purpose, but without the consent, or even the knowledge, of the Lay Impropriators of the Church.

16. - Anonymous Article in the Cincinnati Commercial Gazette, of May 26, 1883, headed "Shakspeare at Home," where it is said "Nor should they [the antiquarians of England] rest until they have explored Shakspeare's tomb. That this should be prevented by the doggerel engraved upon it, is unworthy of a scientific age. I have heard it suggested that if any documents were buried with Shakspeare, they would, by this time, have been destroyed by the moisture of the earth, but the grave is considerably above the level

of the Avon, as I observed to-day, and even any traces connected with the form of the poet would be useful. His skull if still not turned to dust, should be preserved in the Royal College of Surgeons, as the apex of the climbing series of skeletons, from the microscopic to the divine."

17. - Ingleby, C. M., Shakespeare's Bones, June, 1883, being the foregoing essay.

FOOTNOTES:

{1a} The corrigenda has been applied to this eBook. For example, in the book this phrase is "and its ancient tombs" but is corrected in the corrigenda to "and our ancient tombs". DP.

{1b} See The Times, July 14 and August 8, 1881.

{2} Jordan's Meeting-house, near Chalfont St. Giles, Bucks. See The Times, July 20, 1881.

{19} The Life of Milton. London: 1699. P. 149.

{20} Morning Chronicle, March 18, 1799.

{21a} See Notes and Queries, 1st S., xi, 496, and xii, 75.

{21b} See Notes and Queries, 1st S., xi, 496, and xii, 75.

{22} An Account of what appeared on opening the Coffin of King Charles the First in the vault of Henry VIII, in [the Tomb House,] St. George's Chapel, Windsor, on the First of April, MDCCCXIII.

{23} It appears that the examiners omitted to utilize this unctuous mask for the purpose of taking a plaster cast: a default which, as we shall see, has been paralleled by those who conducted other examinations of the kind.

{24} Works of Robert Burns: Bohn, 1842.

{26} Prefatory Notice to Cunningham's larger edition of Ben Jonson's Works, pp. xviii-xx. For other examples, see God's Acre, by Mrs. Stone, 1858, chapter xiv, and Notes and Queries, 6th S., vii, 161.

{27a} 2nd S., viii, 354.

{27b} Ibid, ix, 132.

{29} The case of Dante has been recently alluded to, as if it were one of exhumation. But despite the efforts of the Florentines to recover the remains of their great poet, they still rest at Ravenna, in the grave in which they were deposited immediately after his death.

{31} Traditionary Anecdotes of Shakespeare., 1883, p. 11.

{32} Outlines of the Life of Shakespeare. 3rd edition, 1883, p. 223.

{33} Life Portraits of Shakespeare. 1864, p. 10.

{34} Shakespeare: The Man and The Book. Part I, p. 79.

{35} As to this, see an article contributed by me to The Antiquary for September, 1880: also the Shakespeare Jahrbuch, vol. x, 1875, for Dr. Schaafhausen's views.

{37} There is no engraving by "Dunbar": that name was Friswell's mistake for Dunkarton. Boaden's "absolute fac-simile" and "no difference whatever," (Inquiry, 1. p., page 137) are expressions not borne out by the engravings. My old friend, the Rev. Charles Evans, Rector of Solihull, who possesses the almost unrivalled Marsh Collection of Engraved Portraits of Shakespeare, at my request compared Cooper's engraving of the Croker portrait with those by Dunkarton, Earlom, and Turner, of the Janssen: and he writes: "In the Cooper the face is peaked, the beard more pointed, and the ruff different in the points." After all, such differences may well be the creation of the engravers. I would fain know where the Croker portrait now is; and also that which belonged to the late Dr. Turton, Bishop of Ely.

{39} A Study of Shakespeare's Portraits. 1876, p. 23.

{45} This is exactly as it stands upon the existing gravestone, not as it is reproduced by the writer in the Atlantic Monthly: the like as to the two lines of the epitaph in No. 6. The manuscript of Dowdall, referred to on p. 31 ante, is unfortunately modernized in Traditionary Anecdotes. He has, indeed 'friend,' and 'these,' as in the pamphlet version, but also 'digg,' and 'inclosed.' Dowdall, however, was a very inaccurate copyist. See fac-simile in Mr. J. O. Halliwell's Folio Shakespeare, vol. i, inserted between pp. 78 and 79. The Dowdall manuscript does not give the epitaph in capitals, except the initials.